BIG PICTURE 📷 SPORTS

Meet the
BALTIMORE RAVENS

BY
ZACK BURGESS

NORWOOD HOUSE PRESS
CHICAGO, ILLINOIS

NORWOODHOUSE PRESS

P.O. Box 316598 • Chicago, Illinois 60631
For more information about Norwood House Press please visit our website at
www.norwoodhousepress.com or call 866-565-2900.

Photo Credits:
All photos courtesy of Associated Press, except for the following: The Upper Deck Co. (6, 11 bottom),
Pinnacle Brands (10 top), Topps, Inc. (10 bottom, 11 middle, 18), Donruss-Panini America (11 top),
Sports Illustrated for Kids (23).

Cover Photo: Matt Patterson/Associated Press

The football memorabilia photographed for this book is part of the authors' collection. The collectibles used
for artistic background purposes in this series were manufactured by many different card companies—
including Bowman, Donruss, Fleer, Leaf, O-Pee-Chee, Pacific, Panini America, Philadelphia Chewing Gum,
Pinnacle, Pro Line, Pro Set, Score, Topps, and Upper Deck—as well as several food brands, including
Crane's, Hostess, Kellogg's, McDonald's and Post.

Designer: Ron Jaffe
Series Editors: Mike Kennedy and Mark Stewart
Project Management: Black Book Partners, LLC.
Editorial Production: Lisa Walsh

LIBRARY OF CONGRESS CATALOGING-IN-PUBLICATION DATA
Names: Burgess, Zack.
Title: Meet the Baltimore Ravens / by Zack Burgess.
Description: Chicago, Illinois : Norwood House Press, [2016] | Series: Big
    picture sports | Includes bibliographical references and index. |
    Audience: Grade: K to Grade 3.
Identifiers: LCCN 2015026317| ISBN 9781599537450 (Library Edition : alk.
    paper) | ISBN 9781603578486 (eBook)
Subjects: LCSH: Baltimore Ravens (Football team)--Miscellanea--Juvenile
    literature.
Classification: LCC GV956.B3 B87 2016 | DDC 796.332/64097526--dc23
LC record available at http://lccn.loc.gov/2015026317

288N—072016
Manufactured in the United States of America in North Mankato, Minnesota

CONTENTS

Words in **bold type** are defined on page 24.

The Ravens celebrate a great defensive play.

CALL ME A RAVEN

Ravens are clever and loyal
birds. They don't back
down when another animal
moves into their territory. The
Baltimore Ravens play football
the same way. They always
look for a chance to attack.
And no team does a better job
of protecting its turf.

TIME MACHINE

The Ravens played their first season in the National Football League (NFL) in 1996. Ray Lewis led them to a Super Bowl victory in 2001. The Ravens were champions again 12 years later. **Joe Flacco** was the star the second time around.

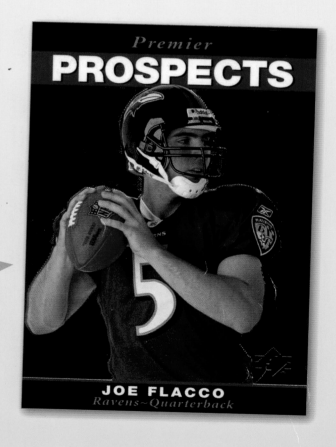

Premier

PROSPECTS

JOE FLACCO
Ravens~Quarterback

Ray Lewis was the fiercest defender in team history.

The Ravens' stadium is a great place to watch a game.

Best Seat in the House

The Ravens' stadium is part of Baltimore's Inner Harbor. Fans can walk straight from a game to one of America's finest aquariums. A statue of Johnny Unitas stands outside the stadium's main entrance. He was the city's greatest football hero.

SHOE BOX

The trading cards on these pages show some of the best Ravens ever.

JONATHAN OGDEN

OFFENSIVE TACKLE · 1996–2007

Jonathan was a huge, powerful blocker. He was an **All-Pro** four times.

RAY LEWIS

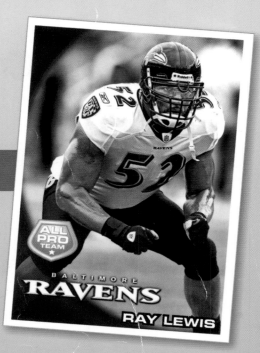

LINEBACKER · 1996–2012

Ray roamed from sideline to sideline to make tackles. He was the NFL Defensive Player of the Year twice.

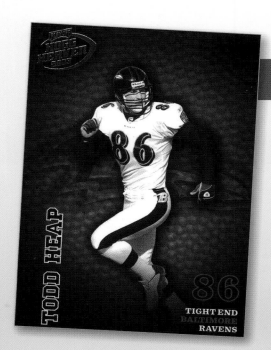

TODD HEAP

TIGHT END · 2001-2010

Todd was one of the most reliable receivers in team history. He caught more passes than any other tight end for the Ravens.

ED REED

SAFETY · 2002-2012

Ed was always in the right place. He returned seven **interceptions** for touchdowns during his career.

TERRELL SUGGS

LINEBACKER · FIRST YEAR WITH TEAM: 2003

Terrell was quick and powerful. No Raven caused more problems for opposing passers.

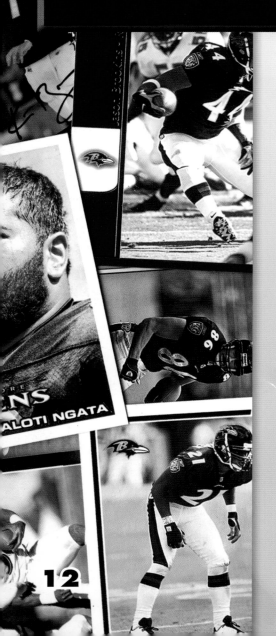

THE BIG PICTURE

Look at the two photos on page 13. Both appear to be the same. But they are not. There are three differences. Can you spot them?

Answers on page 23.

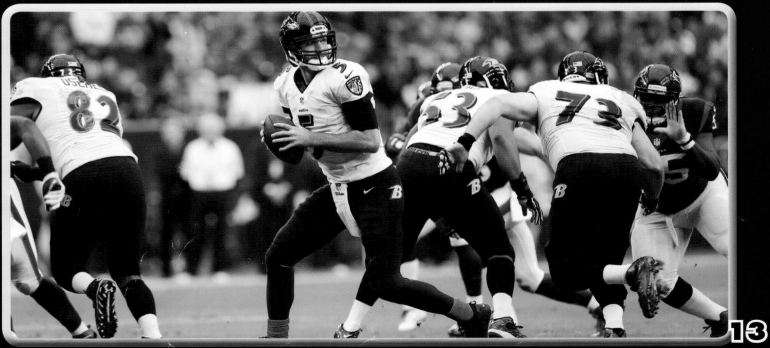

13

TRUE OR FALSE?

Joe Flacco was a star quarterback. Two of these facts about him are **TRUE**. One is **FALSE**. Do you know which is which?

1 In 2014, Joe threw five touchdown passes in the first 17 minutes of a game.

2 Joe has three pet ravens named Edgar, Allan, and Poe.

3 Joe was named Most Valuable Player of Baltimore's second Super Bowl victory.

Answer on page 23.

Joe Flacco looks for an open receiver.

Many fans believe it's good luck to rub the foot of the Johnny Unitas statue.

Go Ravens, Go!

At home games, Ravens fans often show off their singing voices. Their favorite song is "Seven Nation Army." Many Baltimore fans rub the foot of the Johnny Unitas statue before games. If they don't, they fear the Ravens will lose!

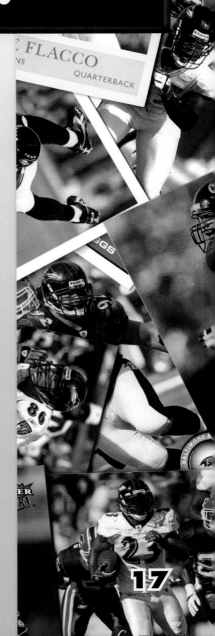

ON THE MAP

Here is a look at where five Ravens were born, along with a fun fact about each.

 1 **HALOTI NGATA · INGLEWOOD, CALIFORNIA**
Haloti made the **Pro Bowl** five seasons in a row.

 2 **TERRELL SUGGS · MINNEAPOLIS, MINNESOTA**
Terrell was the NFL Defensive Player of the Year in 2011.

 3 **JAMAL LEWIS · ATLANTA, GEORGIA**
Jamal ran for a team-record 2,066 yards in 2003.

 4 **ELVIS DUMERVIL · MIAMI, FLORIDA**
Elvis led the team with 17 **quarterback sacks** in 2014.

 5 **MA'AKE KEMOEATU · TONGA**
Ma'ake was the starting nose tackle in the team's second Super Bowl win.

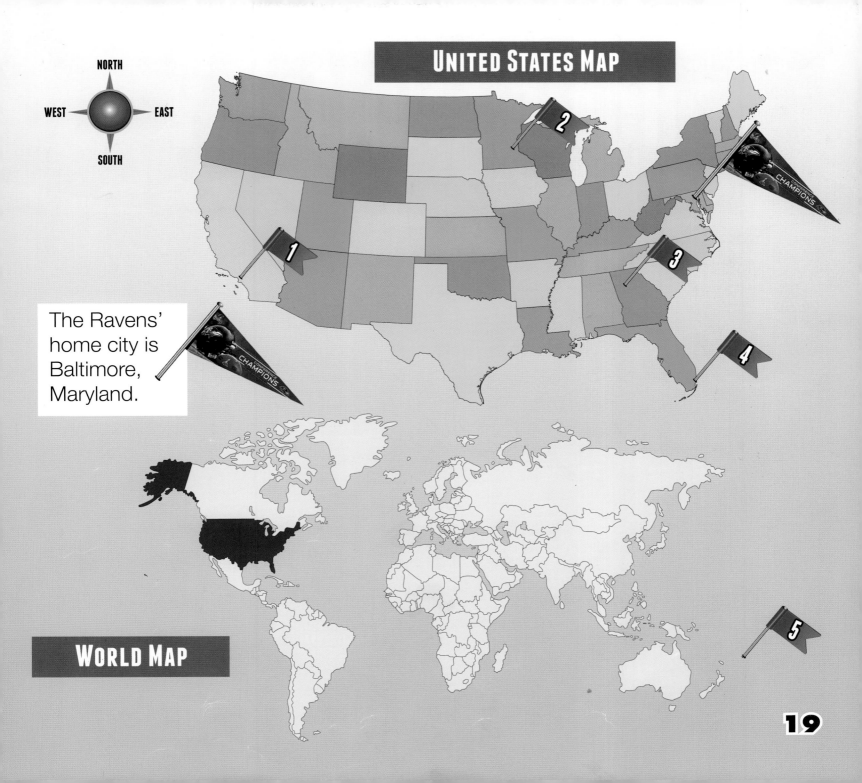

NORTH

WEST ● EAST

SOUTH

1

2

3

4

The Ravens' home city is Baltimore, Maryland.

CHAMPIONS

WORLD MAP

5

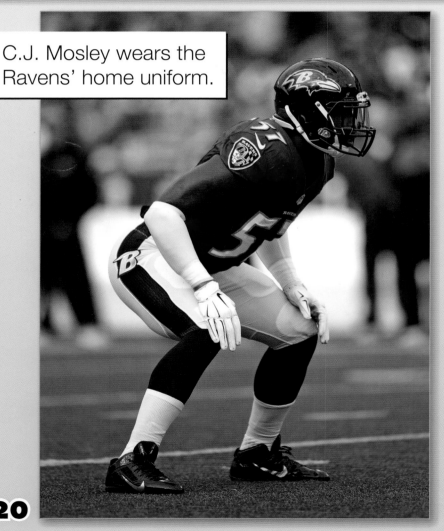

C.J. Mosley wears the Ravens' home uniform.

Football teams wear different uniforms for home and away games. The main colors of the Ravens are purple, black, and white. Black is the color of a raven.

Elvis Dumervil wears the Ravens' away uniform.

The Ravens' helmet is black with purple stripes down the middle. Each side shows a picture of a raven. The team has used this design since 1999.

The Ravens won their first Super Bowl in 2001. Their defense was one of the best ever. Twelve seasons later, the offense led the way. In the Super Bowl, coach **John Harbaugh** guided the Ravens to victory over his brother, Jim. He was the coach of the San Francisco 49ers!

Record Book

These Ravens set team records.

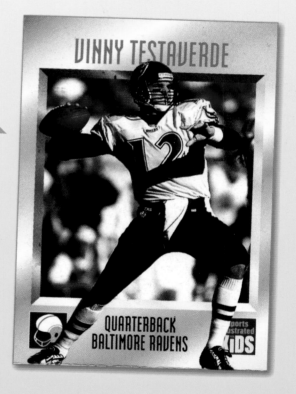

VINNY TESTAVERDE
QUARTERBACK
BALTIMORE RAVENS

Touchdown Passes		Record
Season:	**Vinny Testaverde** (1996)	33
Career:	Joe Flacco	162

Touchdown Catches		Record
Season:	Michael Jackson (1996)	14
Career:	Todd Heap	41

Rushing Touchdowns		Record
Season:	Jamal Lewis (2003)	14
Career:	Jamal Lewis	45

Answers for The Big Picture
#72 changed to #82, the name on #73 disappeared, and the socks on #5 changed to purple.

Answer for True and False
#2 is false. Joe does not have three pet ravens.

FOOTBALL WORDS

All-Pro
An honor given to the best NFL player at each position.

Interceptions
Passes caught by a defensive player.

Pro Bowl
The NFL's annual all-star game.

Quarterback Sacks
Tackles of the quarterback that lose yardage.

INDEX

Photos are on **BOLD** numbered pages.

ABOUT THE AUTHOR

Zack Burgess has been writing about sports for more than 20 years. He has lived all over the country and interviewed lots of All-Pro football players, including Brett Favre, Eddie George, Jerome Bettis, Shannon Sharpe, and Rich Gannon. Zack was the first African American beat writer to cover Major League Baseball when he worked for the *Kansas City Star*.

ABOUT THE RAVENS

Learn more at these websites:

www.baltimoreravens.com • www.profootballhof.com

www.teamspiritextras.com/Overtime/html/ravens.html